Because great leaders know;
a connected team is a productive team.

From the Spotlight to Real Life

Tips From the Stage to Reignite Teams, Spark Communication Skills, and Encourage Speakers

Skydiving will not be mentioned at all in this book.
It's just a cool stock photo of a connected and committed team.

To Marianne,
my TEDx buddy ♡
Lisa David Clark
2023

i

Lisa's book, *From the Spotlight to Real Life*, reads like a road map to success, not only for public speaking but for life in general. More poignantly, and from my experience, her comments and suggestions are also the essential basis for leadership of a successful company. Listening, REALLY listening, trusting, caring, respecting, and believing everyone possesses worth and dignity; allowing each person the opportunity to meet her or his full potential.

Marilyn Moss Rockefeller; Socially Responsible Business Leader, co-founder of Moss Tent Works. Author, Writer, and Philanthropist with a Social Mission. Ms. Rockefeller's Book, *Mountain Girl, from barefoot to boardroom* is not to be missed!

Olson lives up to her title as the "Icebreaker Queen" as she opens her readers to real life tools for building connections in *From the Spotlight to Real Life*. With humor and delightful parallels, Olson will have you hooked from beginning to end. It's a must read for anyone who manages teams or just the average person looking to develop their communication skills.

Cesar Cervantes; Top Talks Coaching, TEDx Mentor, Multi TEDx Speaker, Performer, Speaker, and Speech Writer. Mr. Cervantes helps people deliver their message on global stages, at work or big events.

Contact the Author: lisa@lisadavidolson.com
www.lisadavidolson.com

Cover Designs: Cine1 Productions – Todd D. Olson
Book cover is the author's original acrylic painting
which hangs in the Olson's
living room.

~ Idea to use original art: Mace N. Thomson

ISBN 978-1-73220-592-5 Print
ISBN 978-1-73220-591-8 eBook

Cheesy dedication of grate-itude to all the gouda people who made this book cheddar than I thought it could be.

I thank anyone who has purchased - and plans to read - this book or stick it under the short leg of the table, knowing that I am here to support you. Literally.

I appreciate the ongoing support, patience, and guidance of my superbly wonderful husband, Todd Olson. He is my 'best'. From helping me wordsmith when I can't get it right, to designing the book covers and my card game, to letting me pick on him when I have the zoomies.
♡ I adore you, no end. I didn't even add a pun! That is LOVE.

Thank you to my sons, Trevin, Mason, Sam, Max, and AJ, who never roll their eyes in my presence when I share that I'm working on a new project. You are great dudes who always encourage my wild dreams and I love you all.

A round of hearty finger snaps to those who reviewed my book while in production, and shared reviews for the back cover and the beginning of this book. I am honored that you would take the time to contribute to this rectangle of pages, Jennifer, Marilyn, Cesar, and Drew.

Shout out to my friends and followers for encouraging me to share the randomness of my thoughts and tolerating the unending wave of puns from the sea of guffaws.

Table of Contents:

ACT III
Storytelling Versus Storysharing

INTERMISSION
Stretch, Explore, Discover, Grab Snackies

ACT IV
The Magnitude of One Question

ACT V
Seeking Humor in Your Writing

THE FINAL ACT
A Finale of Fun; Featuring Improv Games
for Your Group or Team

From the Spotlight to Real Life
Tips from the stage to reignite teams,
spark communication skills, and encourage speakers.

We need humor now, more than ever!

I've been told this statement since I started performing, speaking, and coaching around 1999.

The sentence is timeless and ever true: "We need humor now, more than ever!" The reasons vary, but the meaning remains strong, that laughter is a connector, and humor brings people together. We don't have to speak the same language, share ethnicity, or be in the same age group to find a situation hilarious or joyful. And from that shared moment, we connect and spread the fun buzz to our next interaction. It's what I call the Ripple Effect of Humor. This is important to keep in mind as we delve into stage-work tips; how they enhance communication, reignite teams, and spark fresh connections. Using humor is also one of the best ways to grab attention from the stage, and I can't wait for you to learn more about speaking tips to assist you going forward, whether you want to start presenting keynotes, or simply have more confidence with conversation in general.

You're invited!

Imagine being able to strike up a conversation with nearly anyone. Whether you're a leader seeking meaningful ways to connect your team, would like to brush up on speaking and presenting skills, or desire getting beyond awkward small talk in social gatherings. The explorations shared here will entertain fresh ideas toward seamless ways to connect with humans.

Consider the possibility of having a deeper understanding of your work pack, or the gentle thrill of being able to get beyond awkward small talk at events where you don't know many other attendees. I don't know many people who claim to not need a few tips on speaking either from a stage, a desk, or in a small group setting. (Me included, of course).

When I'm coaching someone on speaking or presenting, it's energizing when we land on their golden sentence. The one line of words that encapsulates their message. As a speaker trainer, I am also aware of what I learn along the way with every encounter. That's the magic!

By accepting this invitation to explore ideas from a speaker & performer (me), you are also accepting to:
- Try a dare (or three).
- Doodle on the pages.
- Dabble in creative cues to revive your cemented thoughts.

- Play - to break up the stagnant moments with a current project.
- Explore and find moments that tickle your tummy.
- Take the 'Am I Funny' quiz to see if you are, in fact, funny.
- Glance photos of actual notes that surround my writing space in my home office.
- Trust that you can indeed present information to your work group or from a stage.

For twenty-ish years I've not only been speaking and leading workshops, I've also been writing, producing, and performing in a sketch comedy troupe. Creating a scene, rewriting it, changing it, even *during* the run of a show some nights. I learned to go with the flow and not attempt to alter the river's direction. What I didn't expect to happen with performing is how it would affect my everyday life. Pull up a bean bag chair and grab your favorite beverage. I can't wait to tell you how stage life taught me valuable and useful insight into 'real life'. Whether you are working on reconnecting your work team or social group or seeking a fresh perspective on strengthening one-on-one interactions; this set of pages with words is for you.

In my profession as a humorist speaker and speaker trainer, I had to discover unique ways to deliver talks and work with clients during the pandemic and shutdown of 2019 / 2020. One huge takeaway is that if you are reading this, it means we survived our worst days. The forced reboot taught me the value of not doing *everything*. You are holding this book and reading these words – you're a survivor who is ready to consider dipping a toe further into the creativity realm. Take a quick moment to do a celebratory dance, even in your chair. I'll wait.

Nice moves!
The challenge of the time we live in is that not everyone discovered usable lessons from the pandemic. Being physically separated from work mates, working or schooling from home, extra screen time, and cancelled events, all created fear and isolation. Of course, we also had moments of settling into having food dropped off at the door or never getting dressed in pants with zippers for months on end. If you'd told me a few years back that taking the garbage to the curb was going to be a new fun video to post, I'd have said you need a vacation. But here we are, dressed like a pirate, dragging the bin of recycling to the end of the driveway and lifting the eye patch to yell "Arrr" at the neighbor across the street (who always wears the inflatable dinosaur costume and it's still hilarious).

Consider the feeling of lockdown, and the time it took to sink in to a new quasi-normal. Then how things opened back up and most people were back to the office. It was the 'first day of school' vibe going on. Acclimating to full workdays again was a shock, of sorts. Then we had to actually talk in person, not over a chat thread. The standard "How are you?" with the generic response of "Good, you?" is not going to open a conversation that shares ideas, invites information, or offers true emotion. Ok, you're right, we don't need to add emotion to the workplace. But consider the feeling of a great conversation, one where you learned something worthy of adding the new thought to your mind's suitcase of ideas.

Another win for having a satisfying conversation is when both parties are heard. Not the type of chatter where one voice fills the air and the other person merely waits their turn to respond, but an exchange that includes active listening. This is a paramount skill to have when you are a scene partner doing improvisation on a stage with paying attendees demanding to laugh!

Quick check-in:
You have your favorite beverage, and you grabbed the best spot for reading.
Let's take a deep breath to the belly and on the slow exhale, tell yourself you are ready to receive new information that will Change Your Life!
(No guarantees, but I've always wanted to claim that, and felt this was my best opportunity).

What Great Leaders Know

The best leaders know a connected team is a productive team. Allowing moments of levity or asking general questions of interest are a way to engage your group. Humor has a way of breaking down barriers and bringing people together. In the workplace, it can't be all Seinfeld laugh-tracks. There generally are opportunities of shared times of joy, then getting back to work, which positively affects the next interaction. Including others in on the short burst of humor is also a great way to boost morale and make the day feel brighter.

When presenting to teams, my passion is asking what people do outside of work. Each time I do this, I am amazed that the group who works together doesn't often know personal hobbies of those they are around 40 or so hours each week. Finding out that Sam loves to bake bread, and Tonya volunteers at a dog shelter, are all ways to engage and learn from each other. Give it a try! Having open-ended discussions allows for moments of story sharing, too. This is another superb team building event. Asking follow-up questions, as well as allowing time for anyone who feels moved to share something personal or relatable, is a way to connect and feel heard and / or seen. The return on time investment is invaluable.

Bonus fun-fact:
A moment of humor takes our full attention. To be involved in the fun or to understand a joke, we give it our all. Phones are set down, eye contact engaged, and active listening is on high alert. By nature, we don't want to miss an opportunity to laugh!

According to the Greater Good Science Institute in Berkeley, CA, "Building social connections at work doesn't mean being besties with our colleagues. But when we can see our colleagues as human beings with their own goals and needs, the baseline of social connection, it makes achieving collective goals easier and helps each of us to feel valued, happy, and like we belong."

Teams with connected employees see an increase in productivity of around 25%. Give that a moment to sink in. Fun, joy, happiness, and better outcomes at the day job!? I'll have that, please. After the worldwide pandemic, the shift of how we work affected how we gathered back together after the pandemic. Think about the changes of pre, during, and post pandemic office behaviors.

Even social events that moved to online sessions found it very challenging to get people to reengage in person post pandemic. First, we feared how long we would be isolated, and then we adjusted (as humans do, but forget that we do), and then it was time to find the semblance of a new normal. I still worked in person at the day job, but many nearby office employees outside of my field worked from home. The hardest part about that was the lack of food to sample in the shared refrigerator.

I know plenty of pals who are way less social than before the shutdown. The labor market then realized a record number of people quitting their jobs in search of a new career that would provide more pay, a solid purpose, and (my favorite), happiness.

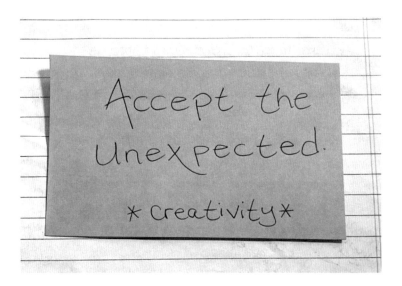

The Ripple Effect of Joy

Whether in the workplace, at a social event, or simply at home – when there is a time of humor and laughs, the next interaction will ride on that joy wave. In the office, we hear laughter nearby and we want in on it. We may even pop our heads around a corner or above the cubicle.

wall (this move is called Prairie Dogging) to ask, "What's all the ruckus?" For two reasons. We are pleased to be able to use the word Ruckus, and because we want IN on the fun!
If we are out at an event, like in a restaurant, and the table nearby is laughing loudly, we look. If you are with me, you will be invited to laugh together more loudly on the count of three. And if you are home and hear laughter in the next room, the chances are great you either go check it out, or yell across the house, "What's so funny?!"

We are drawn to joy; we seek out humor and truly want to laugh. After a moment of shared guffaws, the next thing we do is also infused with levity. This could mean answering the phone with a smile that can be heard on the other end or treating a stranger to a warm smile instead of ignoring them, or not being as stressed at the dog (or toddler) who just made a mess on the clean floor. This is the ripple effect of joy; a moment of levity that spreads like dandelion dust in the wind. Humor is contagious, healthy, and energizing! It raises endorphins, lowers blood pressure, and releases nature's serotonin. Humor also boosts creativity, enhances focus, and increases memory. It's possibly the best hidden healthcare around.

How joy can affect other parts of your day:
- Having a shared humor interaction lifts your mood and the next person you speak with will also pick up that energy.

- Including others in on a fun moment is a great way to increase morale.
- Acknowledge creativity, when two unlikely ideas come together to form a new idea.
- Make sure to bring play into moments organically. Don't force it but do embrace it.

Know Your Audience

As performers, the audience would gather to our shows having a general idea of what to expect because they could read up on our comedy group's history and topics. This means we sort of knew who we had in the room, and that they were there to laugh. Pretty cool. The same as when I am the keynote speaker, I learn about the group who hired me, and I do research on the event ahead of time. But what about in the office? We don't always have the steadfast adoration of an audience member who bought a ticket months ago.

Some articles claim humor to be a superpower, especially in business. Communication is not always about creating laughter; that's a skill left to those who are confident that their audience (or team members) are seeking a humorous moment or topic. As a business humorist, the punchline is one of the best gifts I could give or receive. But it's imperative to *know* your audience. There is a lot of well-placed testing required. Such as sharing a micro dose of gentle teasing or an appropriate joke to see who reacts favorably.

When the timing is right, a message delivered to the workplace with a garnish of silliness can be a wonderful way to create the ever-coveted Memorable Moment. Leaders who can connect the group with a light-hearted way to share information are better respected. But going too far and trying to be Michael Scott from The Office is not going to be the appropriate type of memorable moment. The goal is to find the sweet spot. Humor can lighten a serious conversation, but I recommend caution; as the backfire of bad timing can last a very, very long time. Did I mention I've been married three times?

Humor can:
- Connect teams, whether in-person or online.
- Release endorphins and natural serotonin.
- Ease worries and even anxiety.
- Lower blood pressure and improve respiration.
- Sharpen focus and memory retention.
- Help us feel less stressed, elevate our moods, and enhance memory.
- Build trust and boost team morale.
- Make us more creative and attract others to join the fun.
- Raise the level of admiration for a leader who uses it.
- Encourage collaboration, acceptance, and positive change in the workplace.

With all the superb mentions about the benefits of humor listed above, we could simply watch a favorite comedy to release dopamine. Quick humor dates are not a bad idea at all, because when a person is in a good mood, it's the best kind of contagious for everyone around them. Seeking more punchlines and less headlines is affordable fun. Like gratitude journals, if we were to fill out a notebook with what made us smile or laugh each day, we would seek more fun moments, and you inevitably share them as well. The ripple effect of joy is real, and you could be the Ripple Master. In fact, you could help think of a better name for the person who starts the joy tide. I obviously need assistance in that arena.

Throughout these pages, I'll refer to 'the audience' and ask that you consider a single person you are talking to as an audience of one. Meaning, when it's your turn to speak and perhaps it's you and your supervisor, client, or partner, make that moment meaningful with the tips offered throughout this book. A one-on-one conversation is just as crucial as addressing a football stadium full of fans.

Commit to the Scene

Performers must fully be in the moment on stage and in rehearsal. This means eye contact, active listening, building the scene with cast members and doing everything possible to make the whole show look great and run smoothly. In real life, this means being present when in a conversation or meeting. It is listening to hear the presenter / partner / client and possibly stating back what you heard to show you were present in the 'scene' or moment.

Those on stage are expected to learn all their lines and the physical cues of where to stand, when to move and how to face out to the audience when speaking so they are heard. Have you ever noticed that in a live performance? It's referred to as 'cheating out' and it means you don't fully face the person you're talking to, instead you face outward to the audience so they can 'see' and hear what you are saying. Projecting the voice is also crucial in live performance because an audience that has trouble hearing or understanding what is being said, misses lines that move a story forward and then is distracted by details instead of content.

Commit to the conversation:

- Silence your phone and do not face a computer or other screen.
- Fully give attention to the topic.
- Face the person you are speaking with.
- Speak clearly, and with good intention.
- Welcome feedback and further discussion.
- Once spoken, words cannot be redacted – so have your thoughts 'rehearsed'.
- Keep the conversation flowing by not going back to old issues.

Have you ever been in a heated discussion with your partner or friend, and old issues come up? I sure have. The best way to avoid this cycle is to address matters as they happen, not saving them all up until there is an explosion like opening a shaken soda can. After a few rounds of bringing things up in real time, your relationship will grow stronger, and the walls of worry will not be as high when a deep interaction is about to occur. This is a trust builder.

Listen to Learn

I don't know if you've ever heard this phrase, and it was probably a grandma who invented it; "You have two ears and one mouth for a reason – to listen more than you talk." To be a good communicator, you'll need to master the basics of a solid two-way conversation. Consider the Walkie Talkie. Having only one is not a fully functional way to communicate. Quick question, if you have just one, is it the Walkie or the Talkie?

Listening is a handy thing; for instance, being told directions to the best pizza place, or how to not harm yourself while jump-starting a vehicle. We need to listen to absorb crucial information. The fact is, we only retain about half of what we hear. In the Midwest where I live, we fill in the half we forgot with padded stats and loud adjectives.

The critical skill of active listening is something we must work at. Breaking that thought down is nearly comical. To work at listening? Doesn't it just happen? Actually, nope. Here is an example from performing life; in a scene on stage with one of my comedy partners, we ask the audience for ideas in which to build a sketch in the moment. Think of it as a live version of the Mad Libs game where you fill in blanks to create a scene. Depending on which scene we are creating, we may ask things like, "Name an unlikely sporting event." And "Give me a location where two people may meet for the first time." Next, we establish who we are. We ask the audience for that information as well. "Call out an occupation." Right here is where I will share that nearly every night one bold audience member will call out "Proctologist" as if they waited all day to yell that out in a room of 200 strangers. Good job, Bob. But we, being professionals who are not knew to this idea for an occupation, listen for a fresh idea, especially one that doesn't evoke potty humor.

Standing in the spotlight, with our occupations selected, a location and situation decided from the ideas called out from the audience, the scene begins. As the actors, we have formulas we have worked with for years together. First, we establish who we are right away. This means either my partner or I would open the scene with something like, "Welcome to the t-shirt store, may I help you?" My partner now knows I made myself the shop owner and they are the shopper. Unless they establish a twist like, "I was called about fixing your cash register." And on it goes. We find a conflict to discuss, repair, add humor along the way and find the 'out' to end the scene – with a laugh of course.

Imagine . . .
What if I didn't listen to the audience suggestions and don't know where the scene is taking place? What if my partner

forgets which location was chosen? What if I suddenly realize, while onstage with many sets of eyes on me, that I may have left my curling iron on at home? This is where active listening cannot be taken lightly. I was tasked with asking questions, choosing answers, and making it all work cohesively in a scene in which entertainment and, ultimately, much laughter – are the goal. This is also true for every conversation we have. I am guilty of having a butterfly brain and get sidetracked while I should be listening for the answer to the question I asked in the first place. My husband is so patient with me. Let's just say the computer in my noodle often has all the windows open.

When onstage, I must be focused, engaged, and ready to go forward with information. While selecting answers to use, performers are also considering how to build a comedic scene. It's truly an endorphin rush, and many pals tell me they could never do it. (You already do this when sitting around with friends or family but haven't considered that you are indeed doing improvisation). Woah, dude – how was that for a brain bomb?!

This type of listening, active listening, can become a habit if we make the choice to enter an exchange of information (you know, a conversation) with the idea of listening to learn, not waiting your turn to speak. There are certain people that are simply info-dumping and not interested in your words or thoughts. We have all worked with a person like that (and if you haven't, maybe it was you?) I joke, I tease.

Active listening is:
- Making the choice to listen to learn something new.

- Thinking of a follow-up question to ask the speaker, which shows interest.
- Avoiding the urge to top the speaker's story; collaborate instead.
- Practice - whether at home, at work or school, or in line for a double latte (hold the whipped topping please).
- Check your non-verbal cues; uncross your arms, maintain eye contact to stay engaged. Blinking is good to do to – don't get all weird about it.
- When you ask someone how they are, await a response. Bonus if you ask a follow-up question.

Paying attention to non-verbal skills means our body language is inviting and we are physically showing interest in what the speaker is sharing. If we were dogs, we would wag our tail and maintain eye contact. This would be so cool in a work meeting, but it is said to be frowned upon to leap onto the conference table and wiggle happily. Perhaps there are more professional ways in which to have non-verbal cues for active listening. Consider actions like good posture,

nodding when appropriate (not constantly, that would be weird), setting down the pen instead of clicking it, and a general good energy toward the person sharing information. To be a good communicator, it takes a conscious decision to master the basics of the give-and-take within a conversation. This skill builds trust and is a valuable tool to have, while at the same time opening yourself to receive new ideas. Even if you don't agree with a topic, there is something to be learned within. Even if it's what not to do, it's still a learning. Research has shown experiencing small moments of connection is paramount to team effectiveness. It increases engagement, commitment, renewed energy, and performance. "Small moments matter and can make a big difference to our wellbeing and feelings of belonging." Dr. Kellie Payne, quoted on the Be More Us website.

Speak Like You Mean It

When given the opportunity to present to an event of one thousand attendees, or to your 20 coworkers, or your child's class, or simply at a dinner party; take the moment to share information with the enthusiasm that made you hold these thoughts in the first place. You likely have a passion on a topic, or information you have studied and now want to offer to assist others. Whatever the reason to give a presentation, whether it's a cozy group or a vast event on the center stage, own this moment. Perhaps it's the only time the attendees will ever hear about your topic. Share like it matters because it truly does matter. Give the talk with your heart, because it could be the only time you get to present what you know – and even if it isn't – enthusiasm connects the room and draws the listener in. I think back to high school algebra class, and the monotone teacher speaking of values and formulas and …. I think I just dozed off recalling that style of info sharing.

A one-on-one conversation can still be delivered in a professional, concise manner, leaving room for questions. Keep in mind that we listen with the mood we are in. Just like with texting, we read it with the feeling we are experiencing, and that doesn't always match what the sender intended. If you are stuck in a parking lot with a flat tire, and your partner texts a silly message, chances are you may lash out at them, feeling teased or poked. But what if the other person really means well? As a speaker, clear communication is paramount to gain the trust of the audience. When I say 'audience', this could also be your partner at the end of the day, not always a packed auditorium.

Most audiences will absorb information easier when it is presented in a conversational style. A dash of well-placed humor can connect the energy of the room and put people at ease. Practice being spontaneous. Isn't that a hilarious tip? Sounds like it comes from the school of Oxymoron University. But, just like rehearsing with my improvisation troupe, the topics differ each night and we continually work together on timing, building scenes, trust, and going forward to find the right moment to wrap-up the sketch. The same can be applied to your speech or important talk.

Rehearse the key topics and important information yet leave room to bring in fresh information – perhaps calling back a moment from earlier in the day or something you heard just before you took to the stage or podium. Put in the work to organize your ideas so you can stay on track. That's a gem of a secret that stand-up comics use, too. When they do 'crowd work' which is veering off topic for a moment to chat with someone in the audience from stage – then seamlessly get back into their set list. If you don't notice that moment, they are dang good.

Be open to adapt to audience feedback if you are feeling or hearing it. Don't be shy in asking, too! As I said earlier – what if this is your <u>one</u> moment to be able to share this amazing talk?

⭐ Stay tuned for the upcoming section within these pages that dives further into speaking tips.

Speakers should:
- Be prepared with the points you want to make.
- Practice aloud, record your talk and listen back.
- Have notes if needed, to stay on track - but don't rely on notes overall.
- Include the other person (or the audience) in on the topic instead of talking 'at' them.
- Be flexible in style to mirror your audience and create a comfortable presentation.
- Engage the room in some way, even in one quick exchange.
- Know your audience. Not individually, like where they live, but what are they in this room for? What is the commonality of the gathering and overall idea of why they are here?

If you have stage fright, even for the important one-on-one conversation, take a nature break and work on deep breathing to ground yourself and ease your overthinking. Rarely does a conversation go as we imagine. The same is true for giving a speech in front of a group, or the impromptu conversation about to occur when the boss calls you into their office and requests that you close the door.

Seeking Confidence and Overcoming Nerves:
Feeling nervous before a presentation, performance or a one-on-one talk that has you feeling uneasy is as natural as my hair color (today; not a few years back when I was faux brunette). You are not the first and you won't be that last person to feel jittery before talking in front of a group. But that previous sentence does nothing to calm anyone. So let's dig in a little further to seek how to find our confidence.

Whether you're shy, it's your first major presentation, or you're about to propose – nerves happen. So how do we keep ourselves from simply running away and hiding in a nearby supply closet? First, know that this is not about having confidence or not. Confidence in your topic is what landed you as the presenter. How genuine will your presentation be? Are you reciting words from a slide, or are you able to be You, and add in some stories that are yours to tell?

Keep in mind the nerves and mild panic are from thoughts of what might go wrong, and what could go wrong. This is also called overthinking. If you catch yourself reciting all the gunk, catch that flow and shake it off. You could do jumping jacks and chant, "Positive Thoughts Only!" In addition, or instead of, that fantastic sounding exercise of positivity, you might try what actors do. Being a bolder version of yourself. What would 'Character You' do if they said the wrong word on stage? Certainly not the supply closet idea mentioned above (unless it was a cheeky Adam Sandler movie). The bolder version of you would simply admit the wrong word and correct it, keeping the forward-flow of the talk.

Every single person stumbles on words and thoughts. Just today I walked into our kitchen and couldn't remember why. So, I grabbed some iced tea, took a second and recalled the task. It's relatable. People are attracted to approachable, 'real', people. If you've been practicing your talk, recording it to listen back, and tried it facing different walls of your home or office, you've been doing the homework. Not it's time to commit. Drop outdated stinkin' thinkin' and be nicer to what you tell yourself.

Pep talks to self are allowed.
"I am ready to give this talk." "I am ready to ask my supervisor for a raise." "I am going to give the best TEDx Talk I can give!" "This is MY moment!"

"I don't know why I walked into the kitchen but, I will enjoy a glass of iced tea because I am bold and confident!"
Promise me:
Please promise me you will do this one thing, if you try nothing else; imagine that the group or person you are about to present to wants you to do well and is rooting for you. Because they are and they do. Think of when you go to see comedy or music – you want that group to wow you and do great things. Correcting yourself in the moment is a type of confidence!

You are not judging them; you are craving entertainment! The same applies when you are the one in the spotlight. And if it's not? Make it so on the inside. The moments are fleeting. If we do our best, and experience a multitude of tiny and giant challenges, I think we are doing what we were made to do. All. The. Things.

I Promise! (*Sign Here*)

_____

When is the last time you stood like a superhero? Try the stance (perhaps somewhere alone); legs are shoulder-width apart, hands on hips, chest open and aimed slightly upward. Enjoy a lovely deep breath in as you tell yourself how amazing you are and how the audience needs to hear your message right now. Maybe one day you'll want to do this pose out in the open or even start wearing a cape. If you do, please send me a photo to add to my bulletin board.

When starting to speak to a roomful, open with a great statement, or draw them in with a story. Don't thank the event center or the staff (you can do that later if necessary). You are there to present and be heard, so draw the listeners in. This is also true when having the crucial conversation with a leader, client or someone who reports to you. Our nerves can get in the way and idle chit chat often raises the sweat quotient. Gently get right to the point. It's not a lunch date – it's a time to exchange necessary information and clarify any thoughts that have slipped off track. Setting a professional tone right away also commands the attention of the listener. Not in a jacked-up or cocky manner, but one that shows you are using the time given to cover an issue that needs addressing.

Trust and Support in Scenes

Oh no! The audience of 200 has come in and are seated. The room fills with a slight hum of anticipation. The lights are starting to dim - which means it's almost time to start the show – but where is my scene partner? What do I do? Applause has begun as the curtains slowly part.

There is a fabulous phrase I learned from my hubby, Todd, when we were teaching an improvisation class to 5th and 6th graders.
There is no age limit on this rock-solid thought;
"I don't know what to do. But if I did know, I would do this
_____ ." and you just enter the scene. Trust your gut to know the hardest part of something new is simply STARTING the thing. One step forward, physically, or verbally, creates an opening that wasn't there. Be brave enough to know you've got so much to share, and honor yourself by trying new things.

Okay - back to the curtains opening, and my scene partner is not posed where they were every night in rehearsal, and we are supposed to enter stage at the same time from opposite ends. Curtains open, spotlights shine so brightly you can see dust particles dancing around. I walk out and start my lines. My partner must have been eaten by an invisible octopus or perhaps is trapped in the historic theater's creaky elevator.

The Show Must Go On. I make up some lines to fill where my scene partner would have spoken and suddenly, she appears, running in from where she was supposed to be. I add a couple of lines to allow her to catch her breath, and she picks right up after a believable reason given for why she was rushed.

Perhaps she couldn't get her shoes on, maybe she had a superbly urgent phone call, or her skirt got stuck in the elevator door – who knows? The magic is in the outcome. Making sure the show went on, and always having your partner's back. When we help someone to look good and solidly support them, it comes back to us in so many ways. The scenario above was completely fabricated. But I've experienced instances close to that, where a partner filled in when my face went blank, as I was not completely focused and forgot a line, or who my character was.

Support of your scene partner in real life means believing the person you are speaking with has the best of intentions and does not want you to look bad. An argument can only occur if both parties agree to not agree. Isn't that a wild notion? It's been said no one can make you look bad without your permission.

Support of your partner is:
- Building trust through actions and positive statements.
- Believing the best in the other person.
- Hearing *what* they are saying, as well as *how* they are saying it.

- Making the person look good and speaking favorably about them.
- Covering if the other person has a failure moment, as you'd want done for you.

Avoid defining the end point of a conversation before the interaction even occurs. It's best to allow yourself a chance to use your creative thinking and positivity to be able to land on a successful outcome.

Pivots, redirection, and all kinds of changes are not roadblocks unless you allow them to be. It's a healthy part of the communication process. Set the stage with your scene partner (set the tone for the conversation with someone) by inviting honesty and concerns as topics to clear the air. If it's your life partner or someone you work with regularly, let them know you have their back, want to ensure there is trust between you, and how much their support also means to you.

This works under those spotlights well, and it absolutely will work for your conversations with those who matter.

Use the word PARTY more often!

Have a Laundry Party.
What about a Dentist Appointment Party?
Or Hey! Let's have a Shopping Day Party!
Celebrate taking the garbage out by having
cake when you get back in the house or play your
favorite song to boogie to!

Did this remind you to get the clothes out of your dryer? Party time!

Yes, and …. No

One of the main rules in improvisation, is –

There Are No Rules!

Just joking; there really are some guidelines to creating scenes that make sense, have a conflict to work through, and end on a big laugh.

At least that's the magic formula our comedy troupe worked from. What about this 'Yes, and' verbiage you've heard about in different articles? It's a superb basis for conversation that flows, enveloping listening skills and focused attention, and trust for all involved. This is the most cohesive style of working together in building a scene.

For instance, if we ask the audience, "Give me an unlikely sporting event" and one of the performers chooses the audience member's suggestion of 'cat snuggling', we prepare to create a scene with that suggestion, and build from it. What if one of the troupe members went against the idea in front of the audience? It would be like watching Mom and Dad argue about the furnace temperature.

When someone doesn't use a 'Yes, and' mindset on stage during improvisation, it halts the flow of the scene and does not make your co-players look good. Another example: player 1 is given the name Frank who can't stop his habit of invisible juggling. Player 2 is given the name Patty, who walks up to Frank and remarks, "Frank! It's so good to see you've incorporated imaginary fire into your invisible juggling routine!" What if the player responded, "I'm not juggling, I just like to flap around to add steps to my tracker watch." The. Scene. Goes. Flat.

You knew I was going this direction, but I'll state the obvious anyway. Let's apply the 'Yes, and' theory to conversations in meetings, with our partners, kids – anyone, really. If you are not open to listening to hear, and then build on what you have just heard - this is called a Roadblock in improv stage terms. This doesn't mean you absolutely agree with what is said, rather you won't stop the flow of what is being shared. If you have a gut-burning desire to disagree, using the "Yes, and" process means you don't scream "No way!!". Perhaps you instead gently agree and acknowledge that person's ideas or view (The Yes) then add your own thought, or viewpoint (The And).

You can probably picture the coworker who stops a meeting with the roadblock (No) behavior. It's one of the ways people lose their train of thought while presenting, get sidetracked, and don't experience the team vibe. Support of whomever is speaking matters. You know the feeling of speaking to someone who is pretending to listen. This would never work on stage because it would be obvious as soon as the scene started, that the non-listener was not engaged in taking in new information. The scene would flop and people in the audience would suddenly produce rotten vegetables to zing toward you. Which makes me wonder if people leave fruits and veggies out a week prior to attending a show in case they need to throw it. And if they enjoy the show thoroughly, do they just go home and make a banana bread with the rotten bananas and ketchup out of the soggy tomatoes? I'm guessing you were thinking the same.

Have you ever counted how many times you say 'no' in a day? If your answer was 'no' then you can tally one. Give it a try to see if that's a common response in the workday or at home. Even if it isn't said in a rude way, it's still a roadblock of sorts to keeping conversation flowing. Your subconscious also tracks "no" type responses in the way of assuming something is wrong. Being negative, even gently, creates a tone where nothing is possible, not even going to try (insert topic here). Instead - work on the 'Yes, and' responses and experience an atmosphere where anything is possible, and in the least, not chopped right off the idea block.

The "Yes, and . . . but" is my way of reminding myself and others to not just say Yes when your gut tells you to pause. Example: adding another meeting that could be covered via email. Or running an errand for someone when it is just not convenient for you or your family. "(Yes) I'd like to help, (And) I know this is a need for you (But) as it's not urgent, I need to let you know it would disrupt my schedule right now." Then the other person remarkably figures out their Plan B, and you don't have to be everyone's fixer. Unless I need a coffee.

The 'Yes, and' conversations:
- Allow the other person to be heard.
- Create a way to listen with a focused mind.
- Keep denial out of the discussion.
- Develop a trust, and a feeling of being heard.

- Show you accept what the other person is sharing (this does not imply agreement).
- Invite the speaker to expand on what they are sharing.
- Forward the exchange of ideas.

According to Tina Fey's book, *Bossypants*, "In improvisation - the rule of agreement reminds you to respect what your partner has created, and to at least start from an open-minded place. Start with a YES and see where that takes you." So, if you don't believe me, believe Tina Fey.

Improvisation to Grow Your Business

According the Entrepreneur.com article by senior writer Janelle Blasdel, an increasing number of entrepreneurs are recognizing how improv comedy can bring serious benefits to their business, including new ideas and fresh approaches. Improv can improve teamwork, collaboration, and innovation in the workplace. Use of 'yes, and' technique means team players build on the thoughts of others, rather than shutting down the ideas of their peers by presenting problems and roadblocks.

Blasdel goes on to share that she was an improviser performing in the Twin Cities, and found those skills often paid off in the boardroom, especially for those who are fresh arrivals to a team, new to a career, or trying to launch business initiatives. Following the fear, cozying up to chaos and building trust with coworkers are all tips toward a successfully run office.

What would it look like if you had celebrations for small mistakes? Or accept the curveballs of the day with grace and humor? Your team will be relieved to not have a tense day where more mistakes happen due to fear of reprimand or ridicule. Allowing others to follow the things that make them curious or fearful is the way everyone can learn and grow as a cohesive group.

Jazzing Up the Cyber Meeting:

Screen time has become a (new) normal way to have work meetings, family time, and even doctor or therapy appointments. Let's go over a few ways to add pizazz to online meetings that will hold engagement and make most participants flip their video to on, so they can participate.

Bologna:
Ask each team member to share what they had for lunch (or dinner the night before if this is an early meeting). This is a gentle and easy warm up to get them used to chatting back and forth and maybe even share a recipe!

Props to You:
You'll find a variety of improvisation games later in this book, and many can be played over the computer. One that uses props is fun in a zoom meeting. The prompt is that each

member is going to show off one item from their work area but lie about what it is for.

Perhaps someone has a flashlight but says it's a microphone. Maybe someone picks up their cat (cats are never far from a webcam for some reason) and introduces their sweet little Luci as their boss. You get the idea.

Fairytale:
Taking turns, each person gets to say one sentence until everyone has had a chance.

The leader will start with "Once upon a time" or a similar story opening sentence, and then via hand raise and being called on, each person adds to the story. You could keep it going until a selected sentence chosen ahead of time is reached ("Let's use the ending sentence of 'And that's why Mom never wore shoes again'). Or don't have a set ending sentence, but the leader can chime in with "And the morale of the story is . . . " which indicates you are wrapping it up.

Random Creations:
Using the chat feature, have everyone add a noun. Be thinking of any object, person, or place. A chosen person will view the list and grab two ideas. Next the group will collaborate to decide what new idea will come from the two prompts. Example, New York and Kayaks. Perhaps it becomes a touring company to be able to view the statue of liberty via kayak tours. I'll let you ponder about socks and peanut butter (crunchy style).

Theme Days:
A few days before the online meeting, have a theme for people to dress up in character, the same color shirt, or any type of show you all would know. What if the theme were Pirates, or the show The Office, or Everyone Wear Green, or Hat Day.

It turns out that pants are now consistently optional on cyber meetings, and we are all in agreement to not check.

Bingo!
Play a round of Bingo at the end of a meeting. It's fun to look forward to it if there's a prize. It could be announced that there will be a wild imaginary prize, or there could be an actual prize that's easily sent in the mail or via email (like gift cards).

Mad Libs:
Create a fun Mad Lib to play with the group. This would be done ahead of time where someone writes a work-related story, and includes everyone, then they take out all Nouns, Verbs, Adjectives, and Adverbs. They ask around the screen for the different type words to fill in. I've done this for birthdays and wedding showers. It's always a hit when you read them back!

Share the Spotlight

When a show is in progress, there are several ongoing steps that create entertainment for the audience. It takes a few moving parts behind the scenes so those who are observing can become absorbed in the comedy and / or story.

The best performers do something that, if done right, is not noticed. They share the spotlight.

Allowing your scene partner to be highlighted onstage can also be done in real life. When someone is sharing an event that happened, don't 'jump on their lines' with your own similar story. It would ruin their moment, and it's difficult for those listening to process the first person's story they were sharing. This also builds a trust and the value of being heard.

Remember, if you are forcing your story out to those around you, chances are great your timing is off and it's not the proper moment to be chatting about the amazing night of disco dancing in a pool of vanilla pudding that you recently experienced. (Now 'Dancing Queen' is in my head, along with the accompanying sound of marching in pudding).

Performers onstage are constantly working on:

- The correct lines to deliver at the proper moment.

- Blocking (where to stand or sit, or when to cross the stage at the right moment).

- Making sure to not talk over the others onstage.

- Not standing in front of other cast members, so the audience can see each performer.

- Timing - allowing a crescendo of the audience laughter or applause, before continuing speaking, then picking up lines at the right moment within the energy.

- Getting out of their own way. Let fear guide you, not cripple your thoughts.

Sharing the spotlight in real life terms means:

- Allowing the person speaking to get all the thoughts out of their head, even if it means you feel you may explode if you don't jump in and correct them when they said Maple Street instead of Elm Street! Let the person speaking have the moment.

- Watching body language. Are you jiggling change in your pocket? Clicking your pen?
  Tapping your foot or crossing your arms? The unspoken is as important as verbal cues.

- Knowing when the time is right for you to chime in with your own story. Chances are great that when you wait to speak, your thought is put together tighter, and it will add value to the conversation whether it's a business meeting or gossip on a park bench.

- Being present in the moment. Let the speaker know you are actively listening, from your actions and patience.

- I have a friend who will place fingers on the table or on top of her leg if seated. I noticed this and asked about it. She said, "I don't want to interrupt your story, and I have two things I want to say when you're done." It was indeed two fingers set on the table.

  Not a bad trick!

Quick Break, Brought to You by Our Imaginary Sponsor

Do you stay up late at night, wondering if your friends are charmed by your humor and wit?

Do you think of hilarious social media posts but wait to act and learn your neighbor Steve beat you to it…. again? Ugh, *Steve* – ammiright?

Are you the awkward one at the restaurant table trying to make the server laugh but you receive an eye roll instead of a dinner roll?

Then, my friend, it's time to see if you are genuinely funny, or just *think* you are funny.

Brought to you by Woof & Hoof, perfume for dogs and cows.

"If you've got a stinky canine,
and you want them to smell fine,
or you have a reeky moo,
you know what to do.
Pick up some Woof & Hoof toda*aaaa*y!"

Now, on to the quiz:

The 'Am I Funny?' Quiz

Have you been told you are humorous? Do people put you on the spot and say, "Oooh! Tell this group of strangers about that time you tripped and then made a dance routine out of it. Better yet, reenact it right here – you can finish your dinner later."

This type of interaction means others get a proverbial 'kick' out of you, and that's a great thing. Just not while you're eating and certainly not in front of a group of strangers.

Let's find out if you're as funny as your pals say you are. This is super-scientific, and the final grade matters more than your SAT score.

So, sit up straight, feet flat on the floor, and get a good long sip of water to prepare yourself to learn if you have a funny bone, by taking the quiz that was created by a team of three-toed sloths in the back of an internet café that doubles as a nail salon.

1. What is your preferred method of communication?
   a. Texting. I can't get enough of answering in emojis!
   b. Talking. I want you to stare at me while words come out of my head.
   c. Carrier pigeon. I may not like your note, but I do love to have new friends that fly.

2. What is your favorite style of jokes or humor?
   a. Puns. The cheesier, the cheddar!
   b. One Liners. Keep it quick and witty, with a side of sarcasm.
   c. Memes. If pictures say a thousand words, memes say even more!

3. How do you handle embarrassing moments?
   a. Blame someone else. Denial at its finest, like an artform, or Olympic event.
   b. Laugh it off. Life is short, and it's bound to happen again anyway.
   c. Embrace awkwardness. Own it, wear it, be proud and quirky as heck.

4. A buddy asks you to join them at a new comedy class, and you:
   a. Openly weep. New stuff is scary and there's less danger in staying home.
   b. Study old sitcoms. That way you'll come prepared with tried and tested punchlines.
   c. Run to class. You're on your way, no questions asked, and didn't even put shoes on!

Now we scan your answers through the super-technical tally thingie, and find out if you are, indeed, funny.

Mostly A answers: You are reluctant to share the lighter side and may need to invest in a couple of joke books and take a few pies to the face.

Mostly B answers: You are moderately fun but could loosen up a little more and dare yourself out of the comfort zone. Perhaps walk barefoot while listening to a funny podcast for kicks.

Mostly C answers: You are funny! Now it is up to you to help the others (see previous answers of A and B.) It is the burden of the naturally funny beings to guide the rest into the happy region of ha-ha's and guffaws.

A mix of answers: Good for you, you unpredictable beast! Now that you know you're all over the board on the funny side, perhaps this superbly collegiate quiz will open your eyes and fine-tune your funny bone to the possibility of seeking a little more humor and joy-spreading in your day.

The Right Not to Be Fun

We need to cover this topic to be clear; not every team member in the office or at an event wants to participate in icebreakers, small group activities, or other 'on the spot' games or exercises. When I am the presenter or leader, I remind groups that not every person is required to participate. There are days that even the most outgoing person on earth is just not 'feeling it' and should be met with grace when you figure that out. There are also newer team or event members who need to warm up to the meeting or overall flow of the summit.

Be aware, never force anyone to take part. Don't call people out, like "You! In the glasses and red shirt. Get on up here to stand in front of everyone!" Rather, make it a gentle invitation to see who is willing to participate. Every presentation needs an audience, let the room know it's ok to be on the sidelines, and that when they are ready to participate, there will be more opportunities coming up.

My best enticement is that I always have prizes for those who participate. I make sure no one is in a foolish situation, and I always take the blame for anything that may seem to go wrong. Having a discussion after an activity helps the whole room have take-aways from participating and watching the action.

The LDO promise is that I won't scare the introverts:

We all have those days where we aren't wanting eyes on us. On the flippity side, I usually do have prizes for the participant names to go into a drawing, as a gentle enticement. It's important to let your group know we need an audience as much as we need players and to never force participation or call someone out. That's just not cool.

How we make sure to be mindful:
- Be clear when introducing an activity, that not everyone must participate. If you say this right away, attendees will listen without worry.

- Make it acceptable to bow out of an activity, and let it be an open invitation should they change their mind and want to be included after watching from the sidelines.
- Don't let others pick on those who are not feeling up to participating in the activity. Keep the room as a safe and relaxed zone.

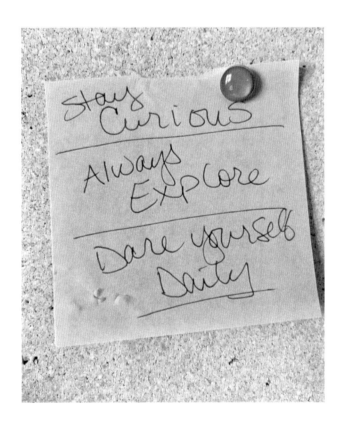

How Improv Improves Communication

Improvisation training is not just for stage performers. It is not even about being funny!

Have you done improv?
You are currently picturing a stage, a spotlight, a microphone, and an audience waiting for you to share your extreme wit right on the spot. Did that make you sweat in the weird places? Life can be like that. But I'll ask another way: do you have a child; did you have parents? A teacher? A boss?

Then you absolutely have done (and do) a form of improvisation each day! It just may not be from a stage for ticket holders. With that in mind, knowing that most conversations are a style of improvisation, you are also like a performer who does not know what is going to happen next. We even improv while driving! That thought is a bit scarier to me and I don't want us overthinking things, so I'll get back on track.

Improv performers accept they are going to be in a scene where the audience will give the idea or premise to play with. It's up to the performers to use the invisible outline of knowing the character, acknowledging a conflict, and finding the 'out' or ending, hopefully one with a hearty laugh track. Now that you know this super-secret format, consider it is in every show you have binge-watched, or movie you've seen. Set the characters and where they are, announce the big dang deal that needs to be repaired and then wrapping up with a conclusion.

Improvisation training, or at least being open to the idea, can:

- Improve our presentation skills.
- Help us drive a scene (or conversation) forward.
- Allow us to follow an idea, using the 'Yes, and' mindset.
- Help us exercise the suspension of judgement by allowing new ideas in.
- Make us more inviting to others who wish to share an idea and shed inhibitions.
- Assist in the art of negotiation and thinking on our feet.
- Open our awareness to how many times we may being saying 'No'.
- Improve communication skills as well as connecting with others with ease.
- Sharpen our skills of being present, focused, and adaptable.

Act II
Speakers Are the Experts

Being the Expert

Earlier in this book, we chatted about speaking to others in the workplace, to a social group, and even at home. Let's go over presentation tips as if you are headed to the stage to give a talk about something you are passionate about, or your expertise. Yes, it sure could be both your passion and your expertise.

If you have been invited to speak at an event, ensure you have all the details recorded in the place you store important notes like personal appointments and your partner's birthday. Track who the organizer is, their title, their contact information, and where and when the event is taking place. This sounds super basic, I know. But if you have the date and time written down – do you have the proper time zone? Some presentations are via our webcams and the silly time difference can make or break a presentation.

If you haven't work with a trainer or coach, I recommend that. Not just because I am one and know many whom I could share with you, but even coaches need coaches. We want to ensure we do the homework to be hired again!

Preparing for a talk is more than rehearsing:
- Be the marketing person for yourself.
- Have a reliable calendar and check it daily.
- Track who you talked with and if they have a team, add their names as well.
- You are seen as the expert on your topic. Act accordingly. Confidence is cool, yo.
- Line up someone to get video or photos of you in action, for your social media and one sheet.

What's Your Problem?

The audience needs your voice, your experience, and your solution. What is the problem you are solving for them? If you aren't clear on this, make sure to chitty chat with the organizer. Speakers are generally hired to fill the spot for continuing education, entertainment, or "Cause Frank cancelled. He's getting a root canal."

Once you identify the company or group's topic and issue, discuss how your ideas may land on a solution. Perhaps on your one sheet or bio, outline your top three talks so the one who is hiring a speaker has a chance to review your offerings and may even suggest blending two topics together. This is good old-fashioned communication at work. Not assuming but asking if you are correct with your plan of action. There are times, during these intake conversations, that I learn of something I hadn't thought of before that could lead to a whole new keynote topic. I'm always listening to what people are interested in. I bet you are, too!

When working with speaker planners:
- Take notes, confirm dates, solidify time zones and locations.
- Get the dates in your phone and set reminders to check in before the date.
- Identify the event's problem or goal for having you present.
- Ensure you have easy to understand tips for the group, and a solid call to action.
- Be a great marketer, share the event if the planners find value in social media.
- Ask about the room where you will be presenting, what kind of mic, and layout of room.
- It's great to talk to the event planner or even visit before the event to check equipment set up and view the space where you'll be presenting.

Nerves Happen

Years ago, I used to teach karate with my first husband (whom I now call friend). I remember at tournaments or just before belt advancement tests, kids would share that they are scared or nervous. One day I came up with a positive response (in my humble opinion it was pretty cool). I'd reply, "That's GREAT!" Which would evoke a wide-eyed stare of curiosity from said child.

I would go on to explain that the feeling is *excitement* and it's wonderful because it means they are going to try their best and have fun!

It's possible I still use this bit of advice when training new speakers. Very possible. ☺

Think about it, nervousness *does* mean excitement! To be chosen to speak is an honor and achievement.
So, prepare the heck out of your presentation. The best way to gain confidence is to be ready and expect that there may be a glitch, trusting you will handle it by being a professional.

I don't usually present with power point slides. One reason is that my style is interactive, and I don't stand in one spot if I can help it. Another reason is tech issues hurt my insides. It's happened several times in my two decades of talking into a mic. Sometimes the equipment doesn't work, other times there is no spare battery for a mic that is going out.

Side note: a major roadblock for anyone trying to address a crowd and be heard is an open bar. People will congregate for beverages and get into conversations. Yikes. It's ok to ask the planner if the bar can be closed while it's your time on the stage.

I find it easier to present to strangers than a group I am familiar with. It can be distracting to be in the midst of a presentation and suddenly you see that Kaylee got a new hairstyle. Or you spot a former coworker that you may think doesn't like you. Then *poof* there goes my thoughts on the topic at hand. This is one reason I have a bullet list of notes nearby. I don't want to rely on my notes, but I do have a hummingbird mentality and just knowing my topics are near if I need them seems to help keep my focus.

Be clear on what is expected of you:
- Be prompt when responding to an event planner. It matters.
- Practice, prepare, and plan.
- Don't depend on A/V equipment. Make sure you have a backup plan.
- Knowing the layout of the room is helpful to plan your stage presence and calm those excited nervous feelings. If the planner is not sure of the room details, connect with the event site coordinator. They probably have photos on their website.
- Always be early. Feel the vibe of the group and the room. Find water. Breathe.
- Believe everyone wants you to do well – because they Do!

Being Perfect-ish

Perfect is like 'normal'. Quite subjective. But nearly perfect is something to strive for when preparing to be the speaker at an event. Now that you know who your contact is, all the details of where, when, and why you are presenting, it's time to shape up that presentation! If using slides, make the font readable throughout the room. Make sure to share the source of your information if quoting from someone else or an article.

Do Not Read from The Slides:
If people wanted to be read to, they could go to Uncle Chuckie's story time at the kids' section of the library. Power Point slides should enhance what you are saying, not BE what you are saying. If the slides aren't needed, skip them. Every one of us has plenty of screen time throughout the day.

Grab the audience's attention right away. Did you know a room of people will decide if they like you in the first 3.5 seconds? That's a stat I just made up. But it is a fact that the first thing you say matters a whole lot. If you thank the event planners, and mention the lunch looked good, the audience already knows this information and will likely check their social media right then and there. You certainly should thank the event planners, but that can wait until the end when you share how people can connect with you.

Open with a grabber sentence. A personal story is likely to get everyone's attention. As a humorist, I prefer something funny to warm the room up. Maybe you saw something unique on the way to the venue, or you have a superb personal story that gets you right into your talk. Work on this. We don't get a second chance to make an amazing first impression.

In practicing your talk, video yourself rehearsing and watch your body language. Never put your hands in your pockets. Don't cross your arms, either. These two moves close you off from the audience. If you can't figure out what to do with your hands, watch TED Talks or presentations to see what you like and what is distracting as a viewer. If you are a pen clicker, do not hold a pen. Also – stop that.

Get the audience to believe in you:

- Some presenters chat with the audience ahead of their talk, casually in the room.

- Do your homework on the group you are speaking to. Add this into your talk.

- Be early, and feel the room, get water with no ice (ice makes noise) and use the potty.

- Always have breath mints in the bag you carry. And tissue.

- Bring a jacket or sweater. Wear clean underwear. (Mom advice never expires).

- It's great to have a give-away item. Stickers, bookmarks, bonuses, and items for sale to connect with the group after you speak.

- Record your talk, even on your cell phone. Not only to reflect on how you did, but also to include any new moments that happened that you don't want to forget.

The Right to Write

You are speaking on a topic that is your expertise. That's fantastic! Do you also have your book written? I'll go forward here as if you do not yet have a book written. Fast forward if you do.

A speaker with a book goes together like two peas in a haystack. Or a needle in a pod. Well, you get what I'm saying. You are speaking on a topic that you know some things about, and now you can write the book to be the full-fledged author / speaker the world is waiting for. The thoughts in your head that tell you you're not a writer, or perhaps the thoughts are ruder; like next door neighbors practicing their bagpipes near your bedroom window at night. Either way, you know stuff. Please share it.

Our inside voice can be quite a troll. When you hear that troll monster telling why you can't, that you shouldn't, it's then that you tell it, "Hold my super-cute water bottle with neat stickers, and watch this! *At this point, you will start to write and quiet the troll voice. Face your fears. Do the things.

Right this moment, there is someone in the world who could benefit from your message and will buy your book. Get the tips, ideas, and thoughts that are uniquely your own, and put them into a book form – we *need* your book!

Find an accountability buddy to check in with so you keep the flow of writing going forward. Hire a coach you trust. It's worth the investment and will save time in the end.

Why you should not put off writing your book:

- If someone else writes a similar one first, you will get very pouty.

- There is a person who exists that is wishing your book was available.

- Being an author is pretty neat and makes you the expert on your topic.

- Books can help a wobbly table be stable when you stick one under the shortest leg.

- You can choose your own adventure – write what you want, how you want!

- Ignore the troll voice in your brain telling you that you can't do it. It's encouragement that you need to get your book out there! Punch that troll in the nose.

- You're feeling nervous? Then do it nervous!

ACT III
Storytelling vs Storysharing

Let Me Tell Ya

If we tell a story to a group, we hope the audience is engaged, listening, and possibly catching the reason behind the share. But 'telling' a story can come across as a lecture. Some might get their phones out to check Instagram and see what their pals had for lunch. Others may rummage through their backpack or purse to clear out expired gift cards and marvel at the number of pens they carry around each day.

If we build a story, we are inviting the audience to join in the creation of the story, or at least add their own ideas and experiences, and this is how we gain trust and tighten connections. We share a moment, and work together.

Stories bring us together and let down guards. They are then remembered and therefore you and your business or talents are remembered, too! This is how genuine and meaningful profit comes through the art of sharing stories. Adding audience input creates value in that they are now invested in a positive outcome. It's groupthink, and a fantastic way to connect.

Perhaps you aren't comfortable requesting audience ideas. That's ok, no pressure! You could include them along the story assembly before the conclusion. Simply asking someone nearby, "Has that happened to you? You try to get ready to leave for vacation and think you packed everything, but realize you only have three out of four kids in the car as you're leaving the driveaway?" Now you have not only that table's attention, but the whole room, as you include people in a question style, instead of just talking in general.

Storysharing is powerful stuff:
- Including your audience keeps them interested.
- Adding attendee input creates a value-added presentation.
- Story goes back to cave dwelling times, it's communication that has stood the test of time. *And I believe cave drawings were the world's first memes.
- Consider the time of year, or trends for your story, while staying true to your brand.
- Business stories should provide a clear outcome; a thought-provoking message with an actionable point to compel the audience to connect with you and your work.

The Power of Storysharing

We can achieve persuasion of sorts with sharing versus telling. Story makes our content relatable. Think of the way we shop. We are generally motivated by emotion. We are told an artist's history or that the dining room table is made from the wood of great grandpa's sloth barn and now there is a rich history attached to the piece.

Stories have been at the core of connecting people throughout history. Your audience is bombarded daily from social media, to texts, emails, and ads in all shapes and sizes. How will you stand out with your business, brand, or as a leader? Knowing your target audience is of utmost importance before you work on the story that is being shared.

Why should an audience care what your company has to say (or you as a brand influencer)?

What is the value you offer to those who work for you or buy from you?

What will make them want to be part of your company or team?

Can you be engaging, yet subtle? No one wants to be yelled to. When someone feels a connection to a company, brand our group, they are much more likely to become a member or customer.

What is something personal about you that you can share that will attract like-minded people?
Hobbies, talents, groups you belong to. It's not about the profession, it's about the person. You.

Connecting through story is a power that binds:
We can be given data (yawn) and proof with slides, graphs, and pie charts. I'll need to pause here and share the curiosity of why there are no cake charts. Stats could be added ala mode style. It's a shame, really. Ok, back on track. Data is

important, of course. But you know what will stick? The story about the dog who was reunited with it's human after weeks apart. We want to know the details! Story engages focus, listening skills, emotion, and excitement for the conclusion....and that's why it is remembered easier than numbers on a slide.

Persuasion, inclusion, connection, and recollection. This is how story will affect the attendees in a large group gathering, or even your coworker, child, or partner.

Selecting a story:

- What do you love? When you share your passion, others feel it, too. It's also how you connect to you 'your people'.

- Find an appropriate story that relates to the topic at hand and has a call to action or lesson in the telling.

- Identify a story where the change you'd like to see has already happened. Learn as much as you can about that situation to compare your personal version to it.

- The more relatable the story is to your own situation, the more believable your point will be, as well as having influential factors too.

- If the story is not an original, credit where you borrowed it from.

- Listeners more easily connect with just one protagonist (main character).

- Practice your storytelling. Record it, listen back. Keep it relevant and not extra wordy. Share with your accountability buddy, coach, or pet. Our dog rarely gives negative feedback.

- Giving a TEDx talk takes your story around the globe! If you aren't ready for the red dot just yet, add story in your social media and watch people more readily interact.

Six Steps of Storysharing

Your audience, whether in person, virtual, or through social media is not 'everyone'.
Before speaking, learn who the audience is. Try to figure out the demographic so you have a general idea of the reason you will stand before them and share words into the air. To assist with this, I now share with you, the six steps of storysharing.

1. Your story for business must be engaging and have emotion.

2. Share your passion, keep it real. You can't appeal to the whole wide world, but you can find your people by being honest with what you know, and what you don't know.

3. Keep content evergreen. When I podcast, I avoid saying "this year" or "last week". It's best to not place dates on topics so that it stays relevant. Be consistent and avoid buzz words to avoid shifting the authentic paradigm and synergy of the tipping-point and off-shoring. I honestly just made myself laugh.

4. Inclusion shows the client that you respect them. By being interactive you not only keep the attendee's attention, but you also make them know they matter. When someone else is kind enough to share with you, repeat part of it back or ask a follow-up question.

5. When planning to speak and have a story at the ready, write freely and write long. Editing later is best so that you can harvest the best parts. When writing a story, include senses such as taste, scent, touch, hear, movement. Go back in the writing – maybe you have more than one story!

6. Overview: step back a bit (in your mind) and see the overview of what is written. Is there a great opening line? A reason to share this story? A moment that will grab the audience's attention? A great wrap-up to end the story with a lesson or a call to action?

Ride a Cloud

You've written a story, or perhaps you have your yet-to-be-written book on your mind. It's great to have notes. Include the steps above. Now mentally step back to look at what you have written. In your mind, imagine the following: you get up from your writing area and stand in the doorway to view the space and consider what you wrote. Does it resonate still?

Next, climb a mountain and sit to view the house or building where you were writing. How relevant does this information feel? Who do you believe needs to hear this content?

See that cloud rolling in? Jump up and bounce into the fluffy floating couch. As you slowly circle around the city where you were writing, do you feel your message is ready to be spread out far and wide?

Can you picture who it is you are writing for?

Does the story still matter? Did the audience change at all? This is okay, but worth noting.

This exercise helped me so much when a coach had me sit with my eyes shut and imagine who I was writing my first book for. It still helps today with a variety of projects and a way to relax. I have a hummingbird brain. I'm interested in ALL the flowers and zoom from petal to petal.

Taking a mental break to realign the Why of my writing, the Who of my audience and the What I crave to share to them is grounding and keeps me on track.

A disruptive concept that has the potential to shift the way we see + do things.

Classic Storysharing:

- Has a great opening line that grabs the listener's interest right away.

- Sharing a mistake that you've come through connects faster than a brag moment.

- Includes great characters of interest. Is there a character who overcame a challenge?

- Will have a thread of commonality to hold the whole story together, not jump around.

- Will have a conflict, something to solve, and what it took to repair the issue.

- Has a favorable outcome, maybe even a Hallmark movie happy ending. (Without the cheesy love triangle); and includes a call to action to get the audience motivated.

- Will get listeners to want to be involved, or even share a similar story with the speaker. That's a win; knowing you inspire and encourage others is what it's all about!

- To identify and clarify your transformational story:
  I used to think _____ but now I'm learning _____.
  I went from _____ to _____.
  I am clearer on this now, but it wasn't always this way (share what your transformational learning was).

Let's Not Say Icebreaker

I'm often asked to warm up a group who is gathered who may not know each other. To be clear, this does not mean 'warm up' as in cuddles and blankies. (Sorry). But rather to get a group to become better acquainted.

The organizer will often add, "But we really don't like icebreakers." Hmmm. That's kind of like saying you're thirsty but don't enjoy liquid served in a drinking vessel. So, when you can't find what you need – you Invent It!

Are you brave enough to step into the **Dare Zone**?

I've created a card deck of fun prompts to encourage active play, storysharing, and even ideas for writing! Each card in the deck has two unique prompts to choose from. Often when I hand them to participants, I give them two cards, so they have a choice of four prompts. It's a more comfortable way to play, having choices.

I've had some participants choose to do the physical (act out) prompts as if it were a game of charades, and they have the audience guess what they are doing. Others have announced the move and gone into it. I usually have a prize at the end, and have the audience vote on the Dare Zone Master. Such a coveted title!

Dare Zone offers straightforward prompts that won't scare most introverts. Those who choose to play, help create new memories and fun stories for later!

If you recall the **LDO Guarantee**, it's that I never scare the introverts, so tell your group that every activity does best with a gracious audience, and those who aren't performing are now the fabulous and appreciative audience.

When we do acts of improvisation and play, neural connections in the brain are strengthened and increase. These are the paths to the brain we use for thinking. The brain is then more efficient in making plans, solving problems, and regulating and identifying emotions. All good stuff when it comes to successful social interactions.

Describe the worst vacation you ever had and be extra dramatic.

DARE ZONE

Be a fierce dinosaur who suddenly becomes happy when it discovers a nearby object.

You're a manure salesman; sell your products to the person on your right.

DARE ZONE

Lay on the floor and imitate a piece of frying bacon, (turkey bacon).

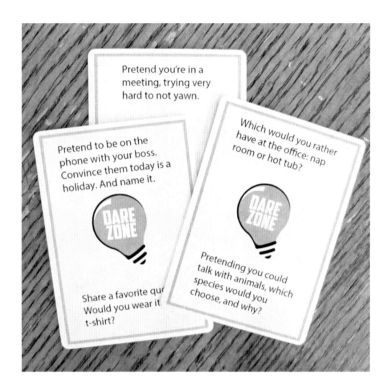

Pretend you're in a meeting, trying very hard to not yawn.

Pretend to be on the phone with your boss. Convince them today is a holiday. And name it.

DARE ZONE

Share a favorite qu[...]
Would you wear it [...]
t-shirt?

Which would you rather have at the office: nap room or hot tub?

DARE ZONE

Pretending you could talk with animals, which species would you choose, and why?

Choose an object or person in the room. Explain how you invented it and why.

Tell us about the super power you awoke with, and how you use it.

DARE ZONE

Be a butterfly who is allergic to flowers but doesn't give up.

DARE ZONE

Tell us about a time when you had horrible customer service.

ACT IV
The Magnitude of One Question

The Issue

Just a smidge of doom and a dash of gloom, here.
We are in a time of unprecedented uncertainty. Due to world events and majorly increased screen time, our ease in meaningful conversation has ridden off into the sunset. Some people panic if their phone rings. It used to be that we got excited like a puppy on espresso if the doorbell sounded. Now we hide and peek through curtains, wondering who in the heck would just show up like that, in person. Unannounced.

Staying Curious

With one well-placed question, we can change our day, a relationship, or even the whole world!
Sure, I exaggerate. Of course I'm over the top with my thinking. Why not pretend we can change the world with our curiosity of others? By showing interest in others, we take in new information. As discussed previously, asking follow-up questions shows we are paying attention and makes the speaker feel – not only good - but also heard.

Imagine being the 'plus one' a business event.
Or perhaps the friend attending a wedding of a family you don't know that well. We have all been there and will be in that spot again at some point. Unless you stay home, order all meals to be delivered and get your mail delivered through a tiny slot in the door. No judgement. In fact, a pizza slice could make it through the mail slot now that I think of it. But you would be missing out on some cool opportunities to learn, grow, expand your social circle, and get invited out again if it all goes well.

Something I adore doing, and even base my podcast – Stranger Connections – on, is seeing what I may have in common with someone I don't yet know. Hobbies, collections, family, travel, work history, all of it!
There is something we can chat about besides weather and sports ball.

According to the Better Help Team, 'Interacting with strangers can be anxiety-inducing, and even downright scary. But these conversations can enhance your confidence, allow you to gain and share knowledge, and start new friendships. In a 2014 study, participants who interacted with strangers while buying coffee reported a deeper sense of belonging and a better mood than those who did not interact with others.'

I like that . . . a Latte! It's about looking up from our phones and choosing to talk with others.

Just Ask

During the worldwide pause, in-person connections were as rare as a finding a 4-leaf clover in a haystack. As an improvisation ninja, I went with a fresh idea that occurred to me while checking out at my usual grocery store.

Cashier: Did you find everything?

Me: Yes, thanks.

Then it could have been the usual pause during the scanning transaction, except I asked 6 words that I've been asking strangers ever since. I am a curious beast, a little bit nosey. (Ok, really nosey) and I love to see how we all are connected.

 The 6' 4", dreadlocked cashier wearing tie dye, paused when I asked;

"What do you do for fun?"

His face lit up with a giant smile as he reached for his cellphone to show me photos of his foster kittens. He leaned down to my lesser height as he told me they are named after the Golden Girls. We Ooh'd and Aaah'd over Dorothy and Blanche who were wrestling a piece of string. Now we're on a first name basis! The employee and I – not the kittens. But that'd be neat, too.

Asking this question is now a regular practice for me! I'm not just nosey, I'm a curious beast doing research! Between floors 2 and 5 on an elevator, the elder man I asked didn't hesitate to tell me that his fun is yardwork and getting fall leaves rounded up. I asked the table of two college students at a coffee house, who answered that they both enjoy writing and are in the same class. The barista joined in the conversation saying she is an avid reader.

A server at a restaurant answered that her fun is her love of insects and drawing them. Then she showed me her bug tattoos. Tattoos of bugs on her arms, not tattooed insects. Though that would be interesting to see.

In three years of asking, no one has ever answered 'scrolling social media'.

What & How

The point is - you can ask this too! At a dinner party where it feels awkward because you are the plus one and don't know many others, when getting your hair cut, at a school or work function, and really any transaction where it is safe to interact with others!

People generally like to talk about themselves. Trust me.
But don't always trust people who say, "Trust me".

My friend Dominique asks; 'What made you smile today?' My pal Martha asks; 'What was good in your day?' Now I ask you what do you do for FUN? We all have something in common. The 'WHAT' is the thing that connects us. But you won't get to the WHAT if you don't ask a question.

Try this question today:

At work, at an event, or to a family member. Don't assume you know their answer. Most of us change the answer often, and that's great. It means we are trying new things. The HOW; if you plan to ask a stranger (in a safe setting) but are nervous about it, is to consider that you are a character of yourself. Like the great actors who seem to be playing themselves in a movie, but it is a version of themselves.

The improvisation thought to putting on our invisible courageous pants is, "I don't know what to do. But if I did know, I'd do this _____." and then step forward and try it. You don't have to be You; you can choose to be a version of yourself!

Take the leap of faith to be brave enough to ask, be wise enough to listen, be bold enough to explore ways to connect. As the saying goes, great things can happen just outside the comfort zone.

A genuine and kind interview of someone you don't know well:

- Shows you are interested in learning about them.

- Gives you an opportunity to discover other interests.

- Feeds the curious zone in our brains, which is super cool.

- Is a chance to network with other people, grow our personal and professional circles.

- Can teach us about ourselves.

- May even make a new friend connection!

ACT V
Seeking Humor in Your Writing

What's So Amusing?

You've done comedy writing. Yes—you!
When your coworker Amy is mocking the office assistant who
is over-the-top dramatic about all that is *The Copier* and you
add to the story, in a Tarantino style, "Yeah! So, the
background of the conference room is blurry-looking and
spinning slowly, and the board members applaud her because
their packets were printed two-sided, and stapled *upper left,
perfect angle*. The supervisor stands and applauds in that
slow-clap style, eyes filling with tears, and says: 'Well done
Kaylee. Well. Done.' "

You both laugh at the absurdity of this.
Now you have insight on how creative freeform thinking
evolves into sketches or song parodies when the comedy
troupe I'm in gathers to create a show. Children have no
problem doing this whenever possible. Pay attention when
the Parent Taxi is in operation. Listen to those backseat giggles
and rants. Kids are always one-upping and topping each other
with imaginative endings that generally include a superhero or
someone getting punched in the ding-ding.

But as we age, we only share our wildest thoughts during
happy hour, it seems. We must totally trust those around us
to truly let loose. Who is that person for you; the one with

whom you can really let go and be silly? If you can't see a face or a name, get on that. To be healthy from the inside out we must land on laughter in the day.

As we age, we lose the belly laughs because all along the way we are told by teachers, parents, and crusty elders, to "Stop being silly" and the dreaded "Be serious." Squish. Smoosh. Flop. What if a class in school included root beer floats and joke sharing for a genuine happy hour; where minds could roam, and silly was celebrated?

What would that look like? To me it would look like a writing session for a comedy show, a safe zone where no ideas are slammed. Where over-the-top thoughts are encouraged and written down. Taking the wacky thoughts and making them workable. That secret formula is also usable in an otherwise boring office meeting.

It's a charming tool I call "Get Your Butt Fired" and it encourages wild ideas, things that would truly get you fired if you did it, like suggesting "Shirtless Wednesdays" and then tone it down to "Wild Wednesdays" where everyone who reached a goal was allowed to wear (gasp) jeans to work. Kind of cool, huh? We will get back to "Get Your Butt Fired" in this book, and you'll have all the details of how to run this game with your own group or team?

The Formula of Funny

Gathering a team at a table to write a sketch comedy show is an open-minded process. Members of the comedy team each have their delightfully quirky humor style that helps to form a sketch collaboratively.

There is a formula to creating a scene in general:

- Establish where we are.

- Introduce the characters and show their relationship.

- Next, a conflict is introduced.

- Once we find a way to resolve the issue, there must be an ending or an out.

- For our comedy troupe, ending on a laugh is the goal every time.

Now you are certain to notice the above pattern in almost every series or movie you watch.

I can prove that you are also improvisation artist.

Are you a parent? Do you have a partner? Do you have a boss? Were you someone's kid?

If you answered yes to any of these questions, you indeed 'do improv' as you make it through your day, just trying to get to the next thing. You may not get paid for these award-winning performances as you answer, "Where do babies come from?" (Generally asked while in a crowded store) but you are indeed a star of the living room couch-stage in that moment.

I invite you to play a game the next time you are checking out at a retail store. Look at the items of the person in front of you as you are checking out. What are the two extremely different items? Now create a story about them to tie together why they bought socks and tennis balls.
What I share during my keynotes is not brand-new science.

Whether you are ready to create a joke book, or simply make the holiday letter more colorful, you should write about things that interest you. Why not try this at the day job, too? Adding humor to meetings or otherwise blah presentations shown on the wall will keep office-mates alert and interested. Obviously, you are promising to keep it corporate clean and appropriate.

What is it that makes you laugh? If you are wanting to add humor to your social media posts or marketing, remember you cannot amuse the world, so writing what you know is the way to attract like-minded people. Consider the last time you laughed at something. Why was it funny? Find more of that stuff. What do you admire about other people's humor? Find a way to make it your own.

Attracting More Humor

Make time for active writing breaks. You know you have at least seven journals you're saving for something. Go get one right now. I'll wait. Now that you have your favorite pen and a fresh journal, add some notes of your favorite humor. Remember to take notes often because sometimes you can put notes together to form a whole new idea for a story, social media post, or work email.

During a writing break, play some music to keep your mood light. Try different styles of music and see if that affects what you write. Research topics to add some flair to your writing. Finding a writing partner is another form of joy for me. Try it! You don't have to be writing a full play to enjoy trading ideas back and forth. But you will land on some fresh and fun ideas that could become a book, a show, a podcast, or a fun story to share with others. Collaboration can be a thrill as ideas form together – it's one of my favorite buzzes.

Write long and write often. It's easier to go back and remove the parts you don't need or want. Never believe the big ol' lie; I'll remember that - I don't need to write it down. When I'm in the car and an idea strikes, I record into my phone or text the random thought to my husband. I've done this so much; he doesn't even ask for clarification any longer. Keep paper and pen near your bed. Don't use the phone at night, because you'll end up on social media buying a squatty potty and you already own three.

How to bring humor to your writing:

- Set down the smart phone and embrace your free-spirited mind.

- Release endorphins and lower your blood pressure through laughter. The more you seek, the more you find!

- Surround yourself with people who leave you inspired and refreshed.

- Avoid the energy vampires who find delight in filling your head with the bad news of the day.

- Collaborate and write with a friend or group to see what humorous or hilarious ideas you can come up with together.

- Get comfy amid chaos. Our brains are idle when not challenged. When it seems there is a lot going on, embrace the whirlwind, then see what ideas or new thoughts stick.

- To quote myself: Seek more punchlines, and less headlines. Like a gratitude journal, you will attract the lighter moments when you are actively inviting them in.

The LDO call to action:

(Read this aloud, with great enthusiasm):

"More Punchlines! Less Headlines!"

Humor Infusion Checklist

1. The Moment
   Choose a scene to work on. It should be relatable, not something that only your family would understand, not an inside joke, but a situation or story people can easily connect with.

2. Don't Believe the Lie
   Write down ideas when you get them. Some quick thoughts in passing can become a whole scene. Do not trust the lie "I'll remember this." Write it down or record it into your phone. You'll be thrilled you did.

3. Rough Outline
   Write your idea out, in a simple format, knowing you will embellish it later. A simple premise is fine.

4. Brain Canvas
   Think about this scene and how to paint the picture for your audience's mind. It is ok to add a bit of flair to make it more humorous. No one should be fact-checking you on what color shoes the subject of this story REALLY was wearing the day this happened.

5. The Set Up

   Check all the angles of the scene. How do you make the characters relatable without having to describe their personalities in great depth? Example: The father is a pun master. You don't have to go into examples of puns while describing him, but certainly come back to that. Dad jokes rule!

6. Call Back

   Be able to circle back to an earlier reference so the readers are now in on this scene, agreeing with what is going on, and feeling included.

7. Find the Twist

   Save the biggest laugh for the ending. Don't give it away in the middle and end with "so there you have it." Instead, write in such a way you have the big punch at the very end.

8. Sketch Bouncer

   Locate a human that you trust will be honest. Read the sketch and see if they react with laughter. If not, find funnier friends. (I'm kidding!)

   If they don't find it funny, ask why and be willing to tweak it.

   Maybe slang verbiage got in the way, or a word is missing and threw it off.

9. Over Do It

   Write often, write a lot, and take the best of the bunch

to work onto stage, your blog, social media, emails, or into your book. Think of it as picking the chocolate chips out of the cookie of life. (Just made myself laugh and now I want a cookie.)

10. <u>Stuck? Grab Tips from Improvisation</u>
It happens. You freeze and don't know how to respond. Using improv skills will help open your mind to new and creative ways to view an ordinary moment. Think wild thoughts. Be a little weird. Or really, really, weird!

Be You!
Then be whoever else you want to be.

We
    only
        get
            one
                spin
                    on
                        this
                            big
                                green
                                    and
                                        blue
                                            rock,
                                                so
                                                    have
                                                        fun!

The Final ACT
A Finale of Fun

Great Leaders Know
The Call Back

This book began with this sentiment, "Great Leaders Know, a Connected Team is a Productive Team", and now I'm going to drive the point not only home, but park it perfectly in the brain garage:

The best bosses are open to hear from their team. They are approachable, they give you time to share and make sure you feel heard. Everyone deserves exceptional leadership, and YOU can be that leader. Let's take a stroll together, to discuss if your team is cohesive and plan to strive to ensure no one feels singled out or not included. It doesn't just happen.

I'm often asked to share games and ideas to help teams to better connect and get to know each other. One way I do this is with the card deck I created (mentioned earlier) called Dare Zone. Another way is to share improvisation games to help groups laugh together. For some reason people run the other way when hearing the word Icebreaker. I believe it has taken on the tone of a screechy voice demanding; "OK EVERYONE! LET'S GET IN GROUPS OF THREE WITH PEOPLE YOU HAVE NEVER MET IN YOUR LIFE."

I'm outgoing, but that sentence makes me sweat in the weird places. There are days I'm not feeling the vibe of interaction. A great leader also knows to not force activities on anyone.

Reminder:
Every performance needs an appreciative audience, so never force people to interact, but do make sure to check in – because often they will take the temp of the room and then decide it does look like something they might enjoy after all.

Coaching the Coaches
Improv Tips for Teams

Accept input from team members:
They are the ones inside the project, work room, or event. It doesn't mean everything is an unending budget with no guidelines. It means to make it a safe zone for new ideas to be considered. Being heard matters. A lot.

If someone contributes an idea that takes hold and moves the group away from the idea everyone started with – let it flow. It's healthy to "Yes, and" or "What If " new thoughts without limitations in conversation. Be prepared to let things shift and allow the overall idea to evolve.

Seek trust:
Make trust part of your team branding and be open that trust and respect are non-negotiable.

Work on some of the improvisation games included here and observe the team in action. Are you noticing good listening skills? Open mindedness? Trust and respect? If not, why not?

Can you let it go?
If someone contributes an idea that takes hold and moves the group away from your own original idea, can you handle that? If it's hard to do this, it is time for a bit of introspection. Is it happening often that it must be 'my way or the highway'? Check in with yourself to ensure you aren't resistant to change. This will gain the respect of your team and make you the approachable leader where people want to work!

Two ears, one mouth:
Don't be the star of every moment. How can you let others be the star? 'Two ears' means we listen more than using our one mouth. Step aside and lead from the sidelines. If you crave a healthy, functional team – LISTEN to those around you. Utilize the people you've brought together. Let the individual talents shine. This reflects well on you, the great leader.

Fail forward:
Mistakes will occur. Is your team able to own up to an oopsie? Is it welcomed to admit a failure or a missed deadline? Here's a secret: everyone slips up. If the leader flips out when hearing of a mistake, they will still happen, but you won't know about it. Let your confidence be seen by everyone, as you gently coach others toward a more favorable outcome in the future. Everyone falls. Not everyone can get back up and feel okay about it.

Let's review a few guidelines before we
get to the improvisation games.
Kind of like having to clean your room before you get
ice cream. *Some things never change.

Be open to ACCEPT your team or group's input:
Your participants are the ones inside the project. Show you
are listening by giving new ideas a chance to be heard. Even if
the idea can't work for reasons out of your control, being
heard matters. Think of new ideas as playdoh. If you leave
them in the can, no one can shape it into something. It just sits
there being sad clay. No one wants sad clay.

If someone contributes an idea that takes hold and moves the
group away from your original idea, go with it. The rule-of-
thumb in improv is to say: "Yes, and . . ." to new ideas without
trying to drag people back to your old concept. Coming in
with a strong idea is great, but if the circumstances demand
for your idea to change and you resist that change, you're
muddy in the water. Be prepared to let go of a single idea and
let things evolve through healthy collaboration.

Say no to saying 'No'. Whacky thoughts should be welcome!
Build team morale by not shooting down ideas. Create a
positive 'anything goes' atmosphere. Even if you hate an idea,
don't say 'No' during the meeting. When your team hears 'No'
in a meeting or even a one-on-one discussion – it's like a door

slam. Then the door is locked and double locked with the chain hook thing, and no one will share what could be the next greatest money saving, time saving, amazing new direction for the company!

#SayNoToNo

Don't build the bridge by yourself:
In a 2-person (or more) improv scene, the outcome is decided together. You don't enter a scene knowing you both will walk out the back door. Use trust by listening and agreeing with your partners to find the outcome together.

Use active listening, agreement, and support to find the end of the scene or the best way to finish a project.

Seek Trust:
Make trust part of your team branding and be transparent that trust is expected.
To create a space that has trust - have discussions and activities to demonstrate you have each other's backs. Make teammates look good. Get to know each other.
Utilize each person's strengths. Celebrate differences.
Honestly support the end goal of a project. If a person is not on board, they should be welcome to express this to the project lead or team director. As a leader, are you approachable?

A scene onstage would crumble if the players didn't trust each other to fill in lines needed, remember your character's name when forgotten or other ways of having each other's backs.

Fall Often . . . get up often-er:
Building a cohesive sketch in-the-moment requires rehearsals, practice, and mistakes of all sorts. You weren't born knowing how to crawl or walk. You fell a lot. You got up even more times than you fell.

Failing forward can be a good thing. As if life were an etch-a-sketch, sometimes a 'do-over' is just what the situation needs!

Warmups To Encourage Open Thoughts:
Before I take to a stage for an improvisation show, I run through verbs. I just start naming all the action words that come to mind. Then I zoom through nouns. I shared this at a speaking event, saying; "I pretend I'm walking through the grocery store, and just start naming everything I see; oranges, shampoo, crackers, salad dressing. It helps to loosen up my mind outside of the thoughts I've had in my workday." An audience member raised her hand and asked; "Which store was it?"

Try:
- Without looking at the paper, stare in the mirror and draw your face without lifting the pen.
- Write the alphabet in slow motion, or backward.
- Create a mad lib story leaving all the verbs, nouns, and adjectives blank, then call a friend or join them on a zoom call.

- Walk in a new area, play different music in your headphones – or simply observe the sounds around you.
- Get low, observe nature from the ant's view. Be childlike and explore.
- Recycle dusty thoughts. Take old ideas and upcycle them!

Friendly Competition
A Plethora of Improvisation Tools Just for You

I'm quite excited to share some of my favorite improvisation games with you. And I'm equally as excited about using the word Plethora in the title above! Pretty cool, huh?

If you have prizes, they will play. I adore coming up with ideas of having fun at work. Of course, play time should not take up work time. It should be in small doses, so the rest of the workday is a sunshiny rainbow of loveliness.

Are you ready to take your team to a better-connected level? Making time for play will pay back with a happier group who will hit ambitious targets, feel valued and will be re-energized. Like I said, if you have a prize, people break out their competitive spirit without hesitation.

<u>Sunflower</u>:

At my day job, a coworker collected five dollars from anyone who wanted three sunflower seeds in the spring. Then he chooses a date in September and the tallest flower wins (with photo proof, of course). I won last year and as of this writing, I am one of the last two with a flower standing (mine is 9' 2" tall.)
This example takes very little time away from the work at hand, and gets people from various departments talking, comparing garden stories, and sharing photos. Fantastic!

Breakroom Story:

Another easy to play activity, is to leave a large posterboard on the wall in a common break area. Have a cup of many colors of markers nearby and start a story at the top with one sentence. The idea is that each employee can add one sentence in their color of choice, until a full story takes up the posterboard.

I used this same idea once for signing a birthday card for a leader. Each person added a line to the made-up story about the boss. Instead of "Happy birthday" written repeatedly, there was a story that emerged which featured a talking chicken who saved the day.

Photo Line Up:

People can be invited to bring in a baby photo or toddler photo of themselves, then have post it notes handy so others can place guesses on who each photo is. Don't forget to include one monkey picture for good measure.

Office Olympics:

There are so many ideas around Office Olympics games! I can offer a few, but I am guessing your own team would love to build on to these as well. Safety first, peeps. You could have speed tying contests – there are sites online that will monitor how fast one can type. Or paperclip chain making races (the loser must take them back apart). How about trashcan basketball or bring in a portable golf set. You could try hallway bowling or even office chair races. A chili cook-off with secret voting, and a traveling trophy for the winner.

Even though you'll offer some wonderful prize, like a lunch or gift card to somewhere local, it's really about the comradery and the fun in competition.

Portraits:

I learned this one from my friend Laurie, and it's a hoot! Teams of two pair up with one sheet of paper each. Whoever is leading the event or group announces that artists cannot look down at their papers when you say "Go". You will give them two minutes to draw their partner's face, but they cannot look down at their paper.

The room will get very loud, and the energy level may even raise the roof. When two minutes is up (or the leader sees that people seem to be done) announce that they should show each other what they've drawn. Have the subject's name at the top and the artist's name at the bottom. This makes for a fantastic display for everyone to view in the office for the week.

Silly Socks Day:

This one was invented when I presented to a security department who didn't have a space where they could do any of the above ideas. We all brainstormed and came up with Silly Socks Friday.

This would only be the last Friday of the month. I worked in the same building as this department at the time and it was so funny to pass each other in the hall on the last Friday of the month, and lift a pantleg to show the silly socks, without event talking.
It made for terrific team spirit and the bonus was how odd that looked to the people who would witness the pantleg lift.

What Do You Like to Do:

This activity is one I made up to be played around the table. It's a great warm up activity. Each attendee's name is at the top of a sheet of paper. Bring markers or pens and pass them around. Each person then writes on each sheet, answering what they think that person does for fun, or as a hobby.

How well do we really know each other outside of work? When everyone is done, pens are down. Each person gets their own sheet back one by one to read aloud, and then they share what they do for hobbies or fun outside of work.
There are sure to be inside jokes released, stories shared, and silly answers that evoke lots of laughs! You can then hang the sheets in the break room or add them to a binder so everyone can review them.

More improv games coming your way after this brief pause
to provide you with a fantastic article about
improv for business enhancement!

Sloan School of Management and is a guest lecturer at Harvard Business School).

"It applies to leadership, and it applies to negotiation, where you never have control over what happens," she said. "Negotiation is a dynamic process - you have to be able to think on your feet and adapt."

Kulhan and Balachandra both said that the key to improvisation is the "Yes, and" principle, and it's an idea they believe is particularly relevant to business.
In performance improvisation it means listening to what someone else says, accepting what they say, and then building on that. In business terms it means accepting any idea that's brought to the table and then taking that idea further.

Kulhan said this kind of "suspension of judgment" is essential for brainstorming and creative thinking, but unconditional acceptance doesn't always come easily to high-flying execs. He said it's not that critical thinking isn't important -- just that it can sometimes get in the way.

"There's a misconception in business that you have to be 100 percent correct 100 percent of the time, whereas the truth is you have to be 100 percent correct about 10 percent of the time -- the rest of the time you have to just make decisions," said Kulhan.
"We get bogged down in analysis paralysis, or just the pressure of being right, and we feel like we have to be

correct all the time. But if you just make a decision, you'll have room to adapt and react and get it to work within the parameters you need."

Kulhan said principles of improvisation can help anyone hone their business skills, and if you can't get to an improvisation class you can still apply the fundamentals of improv to your own life.

"One way is to self-audit - see what you're doing in real time and how you affect other people in real time," he told CNN.

"You can take that 'Yes, and' phrase and test it out at home or in meetings and try exercising suspension of judgment -- try out the principles in real life.

"Through improv," says Kulhan, "we can work on anything from leadership, to influence, to adaptability, to crisis management. We can help people's communication skills. We can show them how to stay focused, in the present moment, at a very high level."

At first glance, zany improv and the strait-laced corporate world might seem to be unlikely bedfellows. But the cross-pollination between comedy and business has led both to fruitful managerial skills development for executives and to fruitful employment for funny folks.

Comedians have not only led training workshops but have begun to infiltrate marketing departments and advertising agencies. They have even, in at least one case, put their stamp on an entire workplace culture.

Article by Mark Tutton for CNN.com

And now . . . more improvisation games!

What 'Cha Doin'?

The game starts with two people on 'stage'. Having two lines of people helps to keep the action going, taking turns joining the scene without being asked. People hesitate if asked.

One player will start by performing some kind of action, small or big, such as pretending to eat. The second person asks person 1 "What cha doin'?".
In this case, person one is still pretending to eat but says something completely different, like, "I'm riding a dinosaur!" Person 2 now takes on what person 1 just said. New person enters the seen and becomes person 2.
Person 1 is still riding the dinosaur. Person 2 says "What cha doin?" and now it's person 1's chance to make up something different, such as "Milking a cow" or "Dancing to rock 'n roll". Person 2 takes on the action and Person 1 leaves.
People soon learn that it's fabulous fun to make the new player do a ridiculous action.

Power Point:

The game pretends to be a power point presentation, but the freeze frame images are when the people on stage freeze on command.
Start with 4, 5 or 6 players on stage. They are in a line, backs facing the audience. The presenter asks the audience for which presentation they are here to see. Some ideas to get them going with calling out suggestions: "Give me an unusual sporting event" "Where was your last vacation?" "Name a 'How To' video you've watched recently?"

The presenter says "Advance" and the players all start to move around. The goal is to always be in contact with another player (this keeps the group tight together). The presenter waits, then says "Freeze".
The group holds very still while the presenter tries to make sense of the scene. Maybe describing (if the suggestion was how crayons are made) that the lead worker is choosing the color while the other workers are wrapping new crayons.
Often, it's a very fun scene and you can have two presenters to take turns describing the scene or chime in with information.
To end, announce that you have one last slide to show them and try to end the topic with the description. Or say that the last photo got in by accident, and say it is a coworker's vacation picture.

Pointed Story:

Have about 5 players in a line on the stage, all facing out to the audience. One person is the director, asking the audience for fairy tales and children's book titles. The fun is in combining a fairy tale with a book title or two fairy tales combined to create something different. You could also instead ask for a silly world problem and a made-up sporting event.
Then ask for a non-related problem to solve, giving an example of, "Like the world ran out of broccoli". Avoid selecting actual news headlines or anything political.

The director's back is to the audience, and they are sitting on a chair or kneeling, so they are not blocking the players. Using a stick or just their hand, the director points to a player and they start the story. The person speaks for as long (or as short) as the pointer is directed at them. There is no limit on how long you hold the pointer to them. Two sentences or a few words is fine.

The director then points to someone else in line – and the first person immediately stops talking even if it was the middle of a word – and the next person being pointed at picks up the word and continues the story. There is no order to pointing or how long they speak. The goal for the players is to work into saying "and the moral of the story is . . ." so the final person wraps up with the ending when pointed to. (Or more than one person can help wrap it up). If it's falling apart and the director has a great ending, jump in to finish the scene.

Going Through the Change

This works well in a large group event. The leader asks people to stand and partner up in twos. There may have to be a couple groups of three, but in sets of two works best. Facing each other, you ask them to observe hair color, eye color, clothing in general. This already raises the energy in the room as it's a bit out of the comfort zone to be so observant with your partner.

Next, ask everyone to go back-to-back. Not touching, just not looking at each other. Instruct the room to change one thing about how they look. You could then play music for this part, but usually it gets loud as people are now laughing and getting creative and silly.
Observe that everyone has done a change, then announce that everyone should face each other and observe what their partner has changed.
They don't expect this: but now you are going to have them go back-to-back again and change something else! Repeat as above.

I generally add a third time (which evokes a fun reaction) and talk to the crowd while they are back-to-back, "Ma'am keep your skirt on please." Or "Wow! I thought your beard was real!" which is silly because they don't know who I'm talking to, of course.
Conclude with having everyone sit, and if time allows, go table to table to ask for the most outrageous change that occurred or if anyone couldn't spot a change.

Learnings are listening, observing, and being brave in getting creative with what they would change to be extra sneaky.

Remember That Vacation?

<u>O</u>ption One:
Ask everyone to walk around the room, then call stop and tell people to find a partner. Now ask the group to pick a location for a fictional trip. Working with a partner, everyone must reminisce about the trip they took together to that fictional location by responding to everything their partner says with, "Yes, and remember when …"

Here's an example of how it might go:

Me: "Hey, remember that time we took that trip to Mexico?"
Partner: "Yes, and remember how we ended up on that deserted beach?"
Me: "Yes, and remember how we found a treasure chest buried in the sand?"
Partner: "Yes, and remember that is was full of gold coins?" etc.

Let the pairs reminisce about their shared memory for two minutes, and then call time. Ask for volunteers to share out the *last line* they spoke. Often the last lines are hilarious, and no two last lines are alike. Debrief with the group how it felt to say "Yes, and" to everything. Point out to the group that everyone started with the same fictional locale, but the groups ended up with wildly different stories.

Option Two:
The attendees are all seated as is usual for the event or meeting. For this version, ask the room to call out where they've been on vacation. Choose one response or combine two answers to end up with something a little silly like, 'The water park at the Eiffel Tower'.

You teach the group that we are all agreeable beings, who will respond with "Yes, and" to the person in front of us, and add to the story. Advise everyone that active listening skills are needed, but not memorization.

Before starting, ask for a conflict, or issue that may have occurred on our fake vacation. The task at hand is to build on what the person in front of you said, along the line the answers will state the issue, attempt to solve it and have an ending by the last person (or the presenter offers the ending sentence).

Notice how saying Yes builds the direction of a discussion, as well as requiring active listening and problem-solving skills (for the vacation issue).

Get Your Butt Fired:

This game is taking the wildest and whackiest ideas and then the room makes them workable. You are also going to learn a lot about your team, because the wild answers can be on the edge of extreme sometimes.

One person leads the ask, announcing that the goal of this gathering is to get us all fired today. Or you can say we are trying to get kicked out of this venue, etc. Invite people to call out ideas that would get us fired or thrown out.

In the past, I've had suggestions of bringing in alcohol, adding a firepit indoors, having a marching band, dancers, drugs, and exotic animals. Let the ideas flow as long as they are being offered. Next, we all take the crazy suggestions, and tone them down to make them workable, so that we don't end up thrown out or fired.

Perhaps instead of alcohol, we have a lemonade stand or root beer floats. Instead of a fire pit, let's make s'mores in the microwave, or have an ice cream sundae station. You get the idea. This game works well because people don't have to move around the room, team up, or interact much. Yelling from our seats makes us brave in the content we share.

Three Headed Genius:

Get three volunteers to stand in the front of the room, facing the attendees. One person is the host. The volunteers will be allowed to speak just One Word at a time.

Let them know the words together must form a sentence, and not just one long string of words.

There can be many sentences, and it will be obvious when a sentence is done. Let the volunteers know you will take turns with who starts each time as well, going down the line with them.

The host represents that of a talk show celebrity, asking the audience what they would like to know from the three headed genius. The host will direct each topic before the ask.

"Does anyone have a question about work for the three headed genius?" Get a question, and then repeat it to the three volunteers so they can ponder their answer. Perhaps the question is, "Why do we only get a half hour for lunch?" The host repeats this to the genius team, and points to which person begins.

They may form a sentence, one word at a time that goes something like this: "Well, that is because we only have four chairs in the break room." The answer doesn't have to make sense, and they team gets better as they go.

Other topics the host could ask the audience might include, Love, Parenting, Hobbies, or Interests, etc.

A B C Game:

Have your group stand in a circle so it is easier to hear each other. Ask for suggestions for a field trip or perhaps different sports or movies. Grab one of the ideas and then point to someone and ask for any letter in the alphabet. Let's pretend they said S. You will start with S and go all the way around the circle in order of the alphabet until you come back to S or get through all participants.

The leader reiterates, "We are going to talk about our Field Trip to the butterfly gardens and begin with (choose a person) and go in order of how we are standing. We start with S, so your sentence will begin with S, first person. The second person will begin their sentence with the letter T, and then the next person is U, etc. Try to continue the story keeping to the theme.

Let them know to think ahead while listening, to figure out which letter they will be using.
Take-aways from this exercise are active listening, thinking ahead and watching what is happening around you (so you know when it's your turn). It's also helpful to tell the group to help the person if they ask for it. Letter X can really be a humdinger!

Creative Thinking:
Take two unlikely ideas to create a brand-new thought, project, or hobby.

Listening:
Using 'Yes, and' to build a conversation. This also builds trust. Listen to *hear*.

Spontaneous Moments:
Explore, add play, seek more punchlines and less headlines. Create!

Inject humor when appropriate:
Lighten a mood, create a connection. Cause the ripple effect of joy.

Take care of your partner / your circle.
Who do you spend the most time with? Is there trust "onstage"?

Do they have your back? Do you have *their* backs?

Do your friends / family know they are appreciated?

How do you show or express this?

Random acts of fun are a must!! Ice cream for breakfast, anyone?

Epilogue and Cast Party
The Conclusion

It's quite difficult to say goodbye, as it is with every show and speaking engagement. It seems we just get used to each other's quirks and phobias, and now we must pick up our props and clear out. But now you have the tools to make a great keynote, the bravery to add your own flair to your talk, and hopefully the curiosity to try out some improvisation games with your team.

I encourage you to stay curious, always explore, share puns freely – even when others roll their eyes or walk away. Puns are healthy for us. (I make up stats and medical advice; never trust me).

Objectives, take aways and parting gifts from your time with *From the Spotlight to Real Life*:

- Trust your instincts. You can think on your feet, you just must make the move to do so. The first step is the right step.

- Explore the limitless possibilities of your creativity. Always try new foods, crafts, games, shows, music, and anything else that will bring originality and newness to your day.

- Build confidence by celebrating every time you choose to try something new.

- Overcome self-doubt in your abilities through improvisation.

- Make mistakes. Fail forward. Predictability is boring. Taking risks will build your confidence and expand your abilities. Some oopsies turn into the best new idea.

- Embrace spontaneity. I'm still working on this one, so let's dare each other to not always have a plan, and just trust that the day will work out as it usually has.

- Explore the fundamentals of storysharing and develop a love of details in your stories. Your characters should have emotional connection in the relationship. Just like real life.

- Meet people where they are, give them grace as we don't know their story. But we can show interest by asking, "What do you do for fun?"

- You don't need permission to play, but I'll give it to you anyway.
- Grease your brain hinges; doodle, dance, play with Legos, paint, volunteer, sing, walk barefoot in the grass, introduce yourself to a bumble bee, pet all the dogs.

- Reflect on your day by acknowledging how truly wonderful the world is because you are in it.

- You matter, and I'm forever grateful that you've read the words I needed to share.

Photo by AJ Olson

Dandelion wishes were made, and here you are!

About LDO:

Lisa David Olson is the (Practically) World-Famous Business Humorist; interactive speaker, TEDx speaker, author, podcaster, and performer who shares how humor saved her life.

A multi TEDx Speaker who loves to guide others to their own talk, Olson is also a speaker-trainer. She brags that she is a professional nag who will help you get your book started or your keynote ready for the stage.

Whether your group is meeting online or in person, wouldn't it be refreshing to connect your team, and enhance communication with a dash of humor? Her interactive presentation style, and tools from the stage to real life, are sought out to re-energize stale thinking. Olson demonstrates how humor is a genuine connector, with a bonus of health benefits!

Game: Her interactive card deck of prompts is called **Dare Zone**. The team building, ice-breaking, fun-making game of prompts! This deck encourages acting, charades, storytelling, and writing.

First **Book:** 'Laughs on Wry' an improviser's memoir. Creative **journal**: "What Ifs and Why Nots"

Podcast: Stranger Connections: celebrating weird life stories and quirky careers (and pranks).

www.LisaDavidOlson.com

https://instagram.com/lisadavidolson

https://podcasts.apple.com/us/podcast/stranger-connections/id1516167809

http://linkedin.com/in/lisa-david-olson-80376612

https://www.facebook.com/lisa.olson.improv

http://www.lisadavidolson.com/

Phun on the Phone – actual telemarketer calls with Lisa!
https://music.apple.com/us/album/phun-on-the-phone/1547231243

Email: lisa@lisadavidolson.com

<u>References used in From the Spotlight to Real Life</u>:

- How Improv Comedy Can Seriously Grow Your Business
  Janelle Blasdel, senior Writer and Content Developer,
  RWR Company

- Greater Good Science Institute, Berkeley, California
  7 Ways to Improve Your Relationships with
  Coworkers

- Tina Fey's book: Bossy Pants
  *(If you know Ms. Fey, send her my way to be on my
  podcast. Thx.)*

- Better Help Team: Interacting with Strangers.

- CNN.com article by Mark Tutton on Improv for
  Business

- Kevin Gilles, artistic director for Dad's Garage, an
  improv and scripted Atlanta troupe

Nosey little bugger, aren't you?
☺